W9-BAU-130

ESSENTIAL LIBRARY OF SOCIAL CHANGE

GREEN MOVEMENT

ABDO
Publishing Company

ESSENTIAL LIBRARY OF SOCIAL CHANGE

GREEN MOVEMENT

by Chris Eboch

Content Consultant

James E. Hickey Jr.
Professor of Law
Hofstra University

CREDITS

Published by ABDO Publishing Company, PO Box 398166, Minneapolis, MN 55439. Copyright © 2014 by Abdo Consulting Group, Inc. International copyrights reserved in all countries. No part of this book may be reproduced in any form without written permission from the publisher. The Essential Library™ is a trademark and logo of ABDO Publishing Company.

Printed in the United States of America,
North Mankato, Minnesota
052013
092013

♻ THIS BOOK CONTAINS AT LEAST 10% RECYCLED MATERIALS.

Editor: Melissa York
Series Designer: Emily Love

Photo credits: Mark Stahl/AP Images, cover, 2; Kim Komenich/Time Life Pictures/Getty Images, 6; Sadayuji Mikami/AP Images, 10; Richard B. Levine/Universal Images Group/SuperStock, 12; Michael Sohn/AP Images, 15; iStockphoto/Thinkstock, 16, 19, 67, 70, 74, 87, 93; Library of Congress, 20 (left), 20 (right); Underwood & Underwood/Library of Congress, 27; Levittown Public Library/AP Images, 28; AP Images, 32, 49, 55; Paul Shane/AP Images, 39; Paul Popper/Popperfoto/Getty Images, 40; Marty Ledenhandler/AP Images, 43; Shutterstock Images, 47; Joe Traver/Liaison/Getty Images, 50; Scott Stewart/AP Images, 59; Fuse/Thinkstock, 60; Paul Hurschmann/AP Images, 65; Gyi Nsea/iStockphoto, 69; Valery Hache/AFP/Getty Images, 79; Charles J. Hanley/AP Images, 81; Tuscaloosa News, Michelle Lepianka Carter/AP Images, 82; Bob Child/AP Images, 88; PRNewsFoto/Newsweek/AP Images, 90; Jose Luis Magana/AP Images, 97; Red Line Editorial, Inc., 100, 101

Library of Congress Control Number: 2013932969

Cataloging-in-Publication Data

Eboch, Chris.
 Green movement / Chris Eboch.
   p. cm. -- (Essential library of social change)
Includes bibliographical references and index.
ISBN 978-1-61783-888-0
1. Green movement--Juvenile literature. 2. Environmentalism--Juvenile literature. I. Title.
363--dc23

2013932969

CONTENTS

CHAPTER 1

TAKING ACTION, ONE STEP AT A TIME

S am LaBudde aimed his video camera at a dying dolphin. It was the fall of 1987. Around him, the tuna boat crew chattered in Spanish as they hauled in the net. They largely ignored LaBudde, but if they had known his true purpose, he might have been in danger. He was working undercover to document the tuna industry's

secret: its fishing methods killed thousands of dolphins
every year.

LaBudde grew up wandering the world. As an adult,
he became interested in protecting the environment and
studied biology with the hope of working in the Amazon
rain forest. In 1987, he went to the Earth Island Institute's
office in San Francisco,
California. LaBudde
hoped to find a job
through the institute,
an environmental group.
While waiting, he read
an article about dolphins
being killed by tuna
fishing boats.

At the time, laws
including the Marine
Mammal Protection Act
contained a loophole.
Although dolphins
were protected by law,
they could be killed
legally during fishing
as part of what was
called incidental take.

EARTH ISLAND INSTITUTE

The Earth Island Institute was
founded in 1982 as a new kind of
environmental organization. The
name Earth Island came from
anthropologist Margaret Mead, who
called our planet "The Island Earth."
She is credited with having said,
"Never doubt that a small group of
thoughtful, committed citizens can
change the world."[1] That concept
inspired Earth Island Institute.

Earth Island Institute began
helping people who had interesting
new strategies for saving the
earth. The institute offers advice,
grant money, and office support.
It backs projects that focus on
changing policies and behaviors.
Earth Island Institute was still at
work as of 2013.

Few people outside of the fishing industry knew how many dolphins were killed this way.

Dolphins and tuna swim together in parts of the Pacific Ocean. Dolphins, being mammals, must surface to breathe air. When tuna fishermen see dolphins surface, they know tuna might be swimming underneath. The fishermen would set nets around dolphin pods to catch the tuna swimming below. Fishermen even used explosives and speedboats to herd the dolphins and tuna into nets. Hauling in the nets captured the dolphins as well.

Although the fishermen were supposed to release the dolphins unharmed, this did not always happen. Dolphins were dragged on board with the tuna and then tossed back into the sea, sometimes injured or dead. Up to 100 dolphins could die in a single net. By 1988, researchers estimated more than 100,000 dolphins were killed each year by US and Latin American tuna boats. More than 6 million dolphins had died over the years.[2] If that continued, dolphins were at risk of extinction.

LABUDDE GETS INVOLVED

Environmentalists had been trying to raise awareness of the dangers of tuna fishing since 1970. Still, the public knew little about the problem. When LaBudde heard about the dolphin deaths from tuna fishing, he told the Earth Island Institute he wanted to do something. The project directors at the institute said they needed photographs. They could not prove dolphins were being killed because cameras were not allowed on US tuna fishing boats.

LaBudde was determined to gather photographic evidence. He went to Mexico and got a job on a Panamanian tuna boat, where cameras were not prohibited. He quickly saw firsthand how dire the situation was. The first catch killed at least 100 dolphins and caught only one tuna.[3]

LaBudde spent close to five months on the ship working as a cook and taking photographs. Finally, with plenty of film footage, he quit in December 1988 and flew back to San Francisco. After editing the videotape, he showed

SPECIES EXTINCTION

Under normal circumstances, species naturally go extinct. The normal extinction rate for mammals is approximately one species every 200 years.[4] By some estimates, more than 1,000 mammal species are currently threatened by extinction.[5] Human activity is a primary cause. Some 180 mammal species are critically endangered.[6] These species are not likely to survive.

Human activity has contributed to species becoming endangered or extinct at this rate. Hunting and fishing practices are among the causes, but humans harm the environment in other ways as well. Many wild lands are converted for farming, logging, mining, or building cities. Tropical forests, which are home to approximately half of all species on Earth, are especially at risk. Thousands of plant and animal species are vanishing every year just from the destruction of tropical forests.[7]

it to environmental and animal rights groups. He found these meetings discouraging. The major environmental organizations were not convinced they could stop the problem. They wanted to negotiate and compromise with politicians and businesses, working gradually to stop the fishing deaths. LaBudde and others from the Earth Island Institute wanted the dolphin deaths to stop immediately. They went back to San Francisco, determined to run a campaign themselves.

The Earth Island Institute sent LaBudde's film to members of Congress and to television stations. When news programs showed the footage, the public reacted to the dolphin slaughter with outrage. Yet many politicians and tuna fishermen claimed such things did not happen on US ships, so laws did not need to change. With no cameras allowed on US ships, no one could prove otherwise.

GETTING OTHERS INVOLVED

The Earth Island Institute found a way to fight back. In the summer of 1988, it initiated a nationwide boycott of tuna. Change did not happen overnight. The Earth Island Institute produced a TV documentary. They recruited activists around the country. These dedicated people

« In the 1980s and earlier, some Japanese fishers intentionally netted and killed dolphins because they believed dolphins competed with them for fish.

Labels on tuna cans indicate whether the tuna was caught according to dolphin-safe standards.

promoted the issue locally, with guidance and advice from the Earth Island Institute. The institute supplied photos, videos, and sample public-service announcements for radio and television. Other organizations that fought for animal rights helped with the campaign.

By 1990, the three major US tuna companies agreed to sell only dolphin-safe tuna. This action dropped dolphin deaths by an estimated 95 percent that year.[8] Legislation soon followed, setting US standards for dolphin-safe tuna fishing. The vast majority of fishing boats now use alternate methods to catch tuna. By 2008, the number of dolphins killed annually in the Pacific Ocean had dropped to approximately 1,000.[9]

Over the last century, people have increased environmental advocacy efforts. Population growth and industrialization have impacted animals, the

THE LOST CHINESE RIVER DOLPHINS

Although dolphins are now in less danger from fishing nets, they still face threats. One species, the baiji, is considered functionally extinct. The small dolphin lived only in China's Yangtze River. Local fishermen once saw the baiji as their goddess of protection.

The baiji dolphins' numbers plummeted due to human use of the river. Dolphins use sound to communicate and navigate. Pollution and the noise of boats may have interfered. Some baiji were killed by fishing practices, including explosions that are sometimes used illegally in fishing. Development projects, especially dams, also trapped the dolphins and limited their food access.

A team of scientists spent six weeks searching for the dolphins in 2006 but found none. There was one tentative sighting in 2007, but even if there are a handful of animals yet alive the species is unlikely to be saved. The baiji is widely believed to be the first extinction of a dolphin or whale caused by human factors. Many other dolphin species are also at serious risk.

wilderness, and even human health. Environmentalists try to raise awareness of these problems and to reduce the damage.

In the case of the dolphins, a small group of people succeeded in making a big difference. In other areas, progress has been slower. This is why environmentalists continue their efforts to change human behavior in ways that benefit the environment. The efforts of these individuals and organizations has come to be known as the Green movement. ●

Greenpeace activists in Germany in 2007 drew attention to »
the fact that 17 dolphins and whales still drown in fishing
nets every 30 minutes. The sign reads "Life is no waste!"

CHAPTER 2

FROM TAMING THE WILDERNESS TO PROTECTING IT

People have been affecting their environments since prehistory. In the early days of civilization, people built towns, roads, and irrigation systems. They cut down forests for farmland, and they hunted and fished for food. Sometimes people managed the land well, but often they used natural resources with little thought for the future. However, before the rise of industry, humans affected the environment minimally.

In the American colonies, European settlers saw the land as an untamed wilderness. Their mission was to reshape the wilderness so it could be better used by humans. Most people saw nature as a gift from God and believed the land and animals were put there for human use. They did not worry about conservation because they did not know they could ever run out of natural resources.

DEATH OF THE DODO

Human activities were contributing to species extinction long before people knew such a thing was possible. One early case involved the dodo, a large, plump bird with wings so weak it could not fly. It had no defenses against predators, but it had no enemies on its home island of Mauritius, which was uninhabited by humans. The first sailors are believed to have arrived on Mauritius in 1507 after being blown off course during a storm. In the following years, other ships stopped at the island. The dodo was easy to catch, making it a convenient source of food. In 1644, the Dutch colonized Mauritius. They brought domestic animals, including cats and dogs. With both humans and animals eating the dodo eggs and young, the bird died out completely by approximately 1680.

UNDERSTANDING EVOLUTION

For most of history, people commonly assumed that every animal species had always existed and always would. Most people did not realize human actions could lead to the extinction of a species. The science of biology helped change that perception. In the 1700s, scientists started studying plants and animals systematically. They collected and catalogued thousands of species. This eventually led to the theory of evolution, the idea that plants and animals change over time. Charles Darwin formalized the theory in 1859. Although many people resisted this theory at first, it eventually became widely accepted.

Scientists in the 1800s also started to realize Earth was

THE FOSSIL RECORD

People did not fully understand the concept of extinction until the early 1800s. A French paleontologist, Georges Cuvier, showed that some species have disappeared. He compared fossil mastodon and mammoth teeth with those of living elephants. They were so different he concluded mastodons and mammoths no longer existed.

Scientists soon began to understand that extinction had been very common throughout the world's history. It is now believed more than 99 percent of all the species that have ever lived became extinct.[1] Species extinction is a normal characteristic of nature and evolution. In recent centuries, however, humans have greatly increased the rate of extinction.

The 1800s brought the first scientific study of fossilized dinosaurs and other extinct creatures.

millions of years old. The geologic record told how Earth had changed. Fossils showed how species from the past had disappeared. If animals, plants, and even the land had changed in the past, they could change again. That suggested human activity could affect nature. The relationship between people and nature began changing.

SHARING A LOVE OF NATURE

Two authors might be called the earliest American environmentalists because of their writings extolling the virtues of the natural world. Ralph Waldo Emerson wrote *Nature* in 1836. This small book discusses what people could learn from nature. Emerson saw poetry and spirituality in the natural world. He wrote,

Ralph Waldo Emerson, *left*, and Henry David Thoreau, *right*, felt a spiritual connection to nature.

> *The lover of nature is he whose inward and*
> *outward senses are still truly adjusted to each*
> *other; who has retained the spirit of infancy even*
> *into the era of manhood. His intercourse with*
> *heaven and earth, becomes part of his daily food.*
> *In the presence of nature, a wild delight runs*
> *through the man, in spite of real sorrows.*[2]

Emerson's friend Henry David Thoreau was influenced by *Nature*. Thoreau built a cabin in the woods and spent more than two years living there. This experience led to his 1854 book *Walden, or Life in the Woods*, which celebrates solitude and communion with nature. In a chapter on solitude he wrote,

> *I go and come with a strange liberty in Nature, a part of herself. As I walk along the stony shore of the pond in my shirt sleeves, though it is cool as well as cloudy and windy, and I see nothing special to attract me, all the elements are unusually congenial to me.*[3]

Thoreau's writings about the beauties of nature inspired many later thinkers and conservationists.

INSPIRED BY TREES

While these authors honored nature as a general concept, something soon happened that rallied people behind a specific cause. Giant sequoias were discovered in Yosemite Valley in northern California. These huge trees towered more than 300 feet (90 m) high. Their trunks could be 90 feet (30 m) in diameter at the base. The Miwok Indians had lived among the trees for centuries. White settlers discovered the sequoias in 1852 and were astonished.

A businessman cut down one of the great trees and took a cross section of the trunk. He thought people would pay to see such an impressive sight. Some viewers did not believe the slices of the tree were real. Others thought killing the 2,500-year-old tree was wrong. People began protesting the destruction of the forests.

Newspaper editor Horace Greeley of the *New York Tribune* was one of those upset by the deforestation. He was also fascinated by the natural wonders of California. He traveled to Yosemite Valley to see the sights. After he spent one day in the area, he claimed Yosemite was the greatest wonder on Earth and deserved government protection. The invention of photography helped spread the word about the amazing sights found in Yosemite, as well as other natural treasures located around the country and around the world.

As the US population grew through the 1800s, people started to see other consequences of civilization and industrialization. Growing cities needed more land and water. By the mid-1800s, the burning of coal was causing pollution in North America and Europe. The challenges of garbage disposal in crowded cities also created health problems. Beginning around the time of the American Civil War (1861–1865) in the United States, a sanitary reform movement had begun to deal with some of these problems. The focus was primarily on making cities attractive, comfortable, and healthful.

PROTECTING THE WILDERNESS

In June 1864, President Abraham Lincoln signed the Yosemite Land Grant. This protected 39,000 acres (16,000 ha) of Yosemite and the Mariposa Big Tree Grove.[4]

The idea that wilderness should be protected was new. Most people believed the forest was full of dangerous wild animals and natives. Forests were being cleared to make room for settlers. Yet businesses and politicians joined naturalists in wanting to protect Yosemite for its beauty.

Eight years later, Yellowstone became the first national park. Yosemite became a national park in 1890. Going forward, the idea that the government should protect wild lands grew.

John Muir was one of the early environmental leaders who promoted the national park system. After traveling the country, he worked in and explored Yosemite Valley. He believed humans to be one part of an interconnected natural world, rather than the masters of nature. This was an uncommon view for his time. In 1873, he began writing articles promoting his ideas and bringing attention to places such as Alaska's Glacier Bay, Washington's

THE NATIONAL PARK SYSTEM

Yellowstone became the world's first national park in 1872. The act of Congress creating the park had two goals: to protect land and to make that land available for people to enjoy. Over time, more parks were created, including nature and historical sites. The National Park Service was formed to administer them in on August 25, 1916. Today, the National Park System has 398 units.[5] These include huge wilderness areas, seashores, Civil War battlefields, national monuments, and historic homes.

THE SIERRA CLUB

The Sierra Club claims to be the oldest, largest, and most influential grassroots environmental organization in the United States. Many of the founding members, including John Muir, enjoyed exploring the mountains of California. Because of this interest, the organization was designed to promote recreation, as well as educational and conservationist goals. Members produced scientific papers and led excursions. Eventually the club built trails and produced maps and guides to help more people experience the wilderness.

The Sierra Club originally focused on the Sierra Nevada mountains and in particular Yosemite. Later, chapters sprang up around the country and began providing their own programs. As modern technology such as the automobile made it easier for thousands of visitors to visit the mountains, the organization's goals shifted. Preservation became more of a priority than providing access to the wilderness. However, the group still promotes the value of wilderness outings. Today, the Sierra Club has more than 1.3 million members.[7]

Mount Rainier, and Arizona's Grand Canyon and Petrified Forest. In 1892, he cofounded the Sierra Club; he would serve as its president for the rest of his life. His goal for the organization was to "do something for wildness and make the mountains glad."[6]

In 1903, Muir took a camping trip in Yosemite with President Theodore Roosevelt, increasing the passion for conservation President Roosevelt already felt. As president, Roosevelt created five national parks, 18 national monuments including the Grand Canyon, four national game refuges, and 51 federal bird sanctuaries.

John Muir wrote an extended public plea for conservation in the August 1987 issue of *Atlantic* magazine.

"Any fool can destroy trees. They cannot run away; and if they could, they would still be destroyed—chased and hunted down as long as fun or a dollar could be got out of their bark hides, branching horns, or magnificent bole backbones. Few that fell trees plant them; nor would planting avail much towards getting back anything like the noble primeval forests. . . . It took more than three thousand years to make some of the trees in these Western woods— trees that are still standing in perfect strength and beauty, waving and singing in the mighty forests of the Sierra. Through all the wonderful, eventful centuries . . . God has cared for these trees, saved them from drought, disease, avalanches, and a thousand straining, leveling tempests and floods; but he cannot save them from fools—only Uncle Sam can do that." [8]

FOR THE BIRDS

The Audubon Society is one of the earliest conservationist organizations that still exists today. In the late 1800s, millions of birds were killed for their feathers, which were used in hats and other women's accessories. This outraged some bird lovers who founded the Massachusetts Audubon Society in 1896. The group was named after John James Audubon, a wildlife artist who had produced a book on the birds of America. Within two years, several other states had Audubon Societies. The groups helped put a stop to killing birds for hat feathers.

The National Audubon Society was founded in 1905. Over the years, the group found many ways to help protect wild birds. Audubon members did not like one old Christmas tradition, called the Side Hunt, during which hunters tried to kill as many birds and other animals as possible. In 1900, Audubon launched the Christmas Bird Count as an alternative. Volunteers go out with binoculars, bird guides, and checklists to count the birds they see. This information helps Audubon and other groups track wild bird health. The Christmas Bird Count is still an annual event.

He also set aside more than 100 million acres (40 million ha) of national forest as federal land.[9]

Many of the first conservationists believed people should manage natural resources to provide the greatest good for the most people over time. This philosophy does not necessarily call for preserving nature for its own sake. For example, hunters worried about the loss of wild animals. They lobbied for limiting the hunting season and limiting the fish and game animals an individual could take.

Preservationists, on the other hand, believe wilderness has its own value,

President Theodore Roosevelt, *left*, and John Muir, *right*, inspired Americans in the early 1900s to protect the wilderness.

regardless of human use. They want to protect nature in a state untouched by people. Wilderness can provide spiritual renewal to people, but wild areas should be left in their natural state, they claim. Muir was an early preservationist. The idea was still largely a spiritual and poetic one. More time would pass before the discussion involved animal rights, health issues, or concerns about future sustainability. Overall, preserving Earth—both then and now—calls for a balance between the utilitarian and the philosophical points of view.

CHAPTER 3

THE MODERN ENVIRONMENTAL MOVEMENT

A fter World War II (1939–1945), industrialization reached a breakneck pace. Thousands of men returned from war, married, and started families, causing a huge jump in the birth rate. As the population grew, urban areas spread out into suburbs. Pollution from factories and automobiles filled the air. Dangerous impurities were found in city water supplies. Yet little was

« The suburb of Levittown in New York sprang up quickly in 1946 with mass-produced, nearly identical houses.

done to protect the environment, and progress largely emphasized economic growth rather than quality of life.

When conservation was mentioned, the focus was on national parks and natural resources. Although science had proved extinctions occurred, it had not shaken the view that humans were more important than other animals. History was seen in part as the story of man's successful domination of nature.

ENDING DISEASE

An example is in the human desire to control disease. One of the most serious diseases worldwide was malaria, which is transmitted

WILDLIFE REFUGES

The 1930s did see some advances in protecting the environment. Sportsmen's organizations from the previous century realized regulating and licensing hunting and fishing was not enough to protect game. Many animals were dying off because of loss of habitat. An important way to protect game animals was ensuring they had places to live. This new vision resulted in the creation of wildlife refuges.

In a wildlife refuge, scientific management helps protect and sustain the habitat and the wildlife living there. When wildlife numbers are high enough to ensure species survival, sport hunting or fishing is allowed on a limited basis. Groups that promote conserving wildlife so hunting and fishing may continue include the National Wildlife Federation (founded in 1936) and Ducks Unlimited (founded in 1937).

by mosquitoes. Malaria infected nearly 750 million people every year and killed approximately 7.5 million of them.[1] By 1950, malaria had killed more people than any other disease.

KILLER MALARIA

Eradicating malaria with DDT turned out to be more complicated than expected. While chemicals killed most insects, some insects survived. Some of these survivors in turn bred offspring with a greater resistance to DDT, sometimes called "super insects."[2]

DDT-resistant mosquitoes grew in numbers, and the malaria rate started to rise again. Changes in farming practices even brought malaria to new areas. For example, clearing forests for farmland can change the local ecosystem, bringing mosquitoes into a new territory. In addition, irrigation can result in standing water, allowing mosquitoes to breed. Due to a host of complicated factors, malaria rebounded. In the 2010s, the disease now affects 30 to 40 million people each year and kills more than 1.5 million.[3]

The World Health Organization is a specialized agency that is part of the United Nations (UN). With financial support from the United States, it started implementing a plan to eradicate mosquitoes. As part of that plan, health workers sprayed buildings with the chemical DDT to kill mosquitoes and other insects considered pests, such as houseflies.

Malaria was not as serious a problem in the United States. But pesticides came to be seen as a valuable and important tool to control pests harmful to farming. In the 1950s, the US Department of Agriculture, along with state and local authorities, started pesticide spraying programs. Sprayed from the air and from trucks, the pesticide was intended to kill insects that could damage crops. What authorities did not then know was that pesticides killed other animals and posed threats to human health as well.

In 1962, the world got a wake-up call. Rachel Carson, a biologist who had worked for the US Fish and Wildlife Service, wrote a book about the dangers of pesticides. If the modern environmental movement can be said to have one literary source, it is *Silent Spring*. *Silent Spring* first reached the public in serial form in *New Yorker* magazine and later was published as a book in its entirety. Carson claimed synthetic pesticides were wiping out wildlife. Across the country, songbirds were dying off in enormous numbers. The loss of their songs inspired the title of Carson's book.

Carson backed her claims with solid, detailed science. Despite all the evidence she provided, many people thought she was wrong. In particular, some in the chemical industry disputed the evidence and dismissed Carson as "an hysterical woman."[4] A spokesman for the chemical industry claimed, "If man were to follow the teachings of Miss Carson, we would return to the Dark Ages, and the insects and diseases and vermin would once again inherit

Many consider Rachel Carson the founder of the modern environmental movement.

the earth."[5] Even the American Medical Association backed the chemical companies.

Others heeded Carson's warnings, though. Just three months after publication, *Silent Spring* had sold half a million copies, and President John F. Kennedy appointed a special panel to investigate Carson's claims.[6] The panel agreed with many of her findings. Bans on some of the most dangerous pesticides began on December 31, 1972.

VOICES OF THE MOVEMENT

Published in 1962, Rachel Carson's *Silent Spring* awakened a generation to the dangers of pollution.

"Then a strange blight crept over the area and everything began to change. Some evil spell had settled on the community: mysterious maladies swept the flocks of chickens; the cattle and sheep sickened and died. Everywhere was a shadow of death. The farmers spoke of much illness among their families. In the town the doctors had become more and more puzzled by new kinds of sickness appearing among their patients. There had been several sudden and unexplained deaths, not only among adults but even among children, who would be stricken suddenly while at play and die within a few hours.

There was a strange stillness. The birds, for example—where had they gone?"

EXPLAINING ECOLOGY

Carson's influence went beyond limiting pesticide use. She explained the concept of ecology, how people and all other living things are connected to each other and to their habitats. The pesticides killed birds because the birds ate insects poisoned by sprayed pesticides. Larger animals, including pet cats, could eat the birds and also be poisoned. Because everything in the natural world is linked, human interference could disrupt the balance of nature. For the first time, people realized technological advancement and

DDT WORLDWIDE

Although the findings of *Silent Spring* eventually stopped the use of DDT in the United States, the ban did not stop US companies from producing the chemical. DDT sales continued in countries that did not ban the pesticide. US companies exported 552 million pounds (250 million kg) of various pesticides just in 1976.[8]

In June 1982, the last chemical company stopped producing DDT in the United States, in part because of the difficulty of competing with foreign companies. Several European and Asian companies still produce DDT.

Today, some countries use DDT in limited ways to combat malaria. DDT use remains a dilemma for these countries. On the one hand, it is one of the best ways to control mosquitoes and prevent malaria deaths. On the other hand, it is bad for human and environmental health. More research is needed to develop a strong alternative to DDT to control mosquitoes and reduce malaria infections.

economic growth were not free of drawbacks. Many grassroots environmental organizations began forming.

The government became involved as well. In 1969, Congress passed the National Environmental Policy Act (NEPA). The purpose of the act was to "create and maintain conditions under which man and nature can exist in productive harmony . . . [and to] assure for all Americans safe, healthful, productive, aesthetically and culturally pleasing surroundings."[9] As a result of NEPA, federal agencies are required to submit environmental impact statements exploring the possible consequences of any major new projects.

SAVING THE PEREGRINE

DDT has killed many birds. Some of the most vulnerable have been birds of prey, which built up huge levels of DDT from eating rodents and other animals exposed to the chemical. Some birds died after ingesting DDT directly. Exposure to DDT also thinned eggshells, preventing the birth of chicks.

The Peregrine Fund was founded in 1970 by people who kept falcons for sport. The group bred falcons in captivity and released them into the wild. Eventually they released more than 4,000 falcons into the wild to replenish the species.[10] This effort together with a DDT ban was so successful the peregrine falcon was removed from the US endangered species list in 1999.

The Peregrine Fund continues today with the goal of saving birds of prey from extinction. Shooting, poisoning, and loss of habitat threaten these birds. They can also die from lead poisoning after eating animals shot by hunters with lead ammunition.

A DAY FOR THE EARTH

Environmental awareness started reaching the general public. Senator Gaylord Nelson of Wisconsin proposed a nationwide grassroots demonstration about the environment. Motivated by the damage caused by a massive oil spill in California, he announced plans for "a national teach-in on the environment."[11] Nelson's idea became Earth Day.

The first Earth Day was held on April 22, 1970. Twenty million Americans took part in rallies across the country.[12] Thousands of colleges and universities organized protests against environmental destruction. Many small groups working for various causes realized they were part of a larger movement. That first Earth Day had wide support, from people from all walks of life and both major political parties.

During the Earth Day ceremonies, Senator Nelson declared,

> *Our goal is an environment of decency, quality, and mutual respect for all other human creatures and for all living creatures. . . . The battle to restore a proper relationship between man and his environment, between man and other living creatures will require a long, sustained, political, moral, ethical, and financial commitment far beyond any effort made before.*[13]

In December 1970, the US Environmental Protection Agency (EPA) was established to carry out NEPA. The goal was to make a single agency responsible for environmental concerns. Priorities included funding federal research on the dangers of pollution and how to control it, as well as setting and enforcing national environmental protection standards.

In the following years, environmental consciousness became a standard part of private, business, and government discussions. Local and federal governments passed legislation such as the

ENVIRONMENTAL PROTECTION AGENCY

The US Environmental Protection Agency (EPA) was established on December 2, 1970. From the start, the EPA faced great challenges. The first administrator, William D. Ruckelshaus, said, "We thought we had technologies that could control pollutants . . . and that the only things missing in the equation were national standards and a strong enforcement effort. All of the nation's early environmental laws reflected these assumptions, and every one of these assumptions is wrong."[14]

However, the EPA has done much to protect the environment. The EPA sets national standards that are then enforced through the states and Native American tribes. It helps implement Congress's environmental laws by writing and enforcing specific regulations. The EPA also gives grants to environmental programs, studies environmental issues, and teaches people about the environment. It plays a key role in defining pollutants and regulating the introduction of pollution into the environment.

Clean Air Act, the Clean Water Act, and the Endangered Species Act.

The Clean Air Act, signed by President Richard Nixon on December 31, 1970, regulates air emissions. The law allows the EPA to establish air-quality standards to protect public health and welfare. States created plans for industries such as chemical plants, steel mills, and utilities to achieve these standards. Since many areas failed to meet the original 1975 deadlines, the act was amended in 1977 and 1990 to set new dates for compliance. The 1990 amendments also gave the EPA more authority to make and enforce regulations reducing air pollution.

The Clean Water Act of 1972 was based on an earlier Federal Water Pollution Control Act. The 1972 amendments allowed the EPA to set water quality standards and regulate pollutants discharged into US waters. The act also funded the construction of sewage treatment plants. Over the years, additional amendments and other laws supported the Clean Water Act.

The Endangered Species Act, signed on December 28, 1973, focuses on the conservation of threatened and endangered plants and animals and their habitats. The US Fish and Wildlife Service and the US National Oceanic and Atmospheric Administration Fisheries Service are the primary agencies overseeing the act. These groups work with other federal agencies to ensure the protection of

High school students in Shorewood, Wisconsin, observe the first Earth Day in 1970 by cleaning up the Milwaukee River.

species ranging from mammals to insects and grasses to trees. With these laws giving the government power to protect the air, water, land, and living species, the modern environmental movement was underway.

CHAPTER 4

GREEN GOES GLOBAL

The 1970s saw the environmental movement take hold worldwide. Also during this decade, the term *green* began to be used for organizations and policies with an environmental focus. The 1972 UN Stockholm Conference on the Human Environment further marked the globalization of the environmental movement. Representatives from 114 countries attended the June conference, along with representatives of governmental and nongovernmental organizations.[1] An important consensus emerged: environmental problems reached worldwide and therefore needed a global approach. This led to a list of environmental policy goals and objectives known as the Stockholm Declaration. The declaration acknowledged each country's right to make use of its own natural resources. However, each country had "the responsibility to ensure that activities within their jurisdiction or control do not cause damage to the environment" outside their borders.[2]

The environmental movement spread as more countries started their own national environmental agencies similar to the EPA. Between 1972 and 1982, the number of these agencies increased from 26 to 144.[3] Despite this growing awareness,

CHEMICALS CROSSING BORDERS

The movement of poisonous chemicals through ecosystems is one example that shows environmental problems are global problems. Chemicals ignore national boundaries. Chemicals such as DDT travel through rivers, lakes, and oceans. They can also cross borders when exposed produce grown in other countries is transported. This may lead to health problems even in countries that have banned the chemicals. In 1972, there were an estimated 500,000 cases of accidental pesticide poisoning worldwide. By 1990, the numbers were between 3.5 and 5 million, with more than 20,000 deaths.[4]

environmental progress suffered setbacks. In the United States, the 1970s saw economic stagnation, high unemployment rates, and inflation. When the EPA forced chemical companies to stop selling dangerous chemicals in the United States, some companies moved their research and production to other countries. Some blamed the EPA for the loss of jobs at home.

At the same time, pesticides were still seen as the best way to increase food production. Without chemical solutions, people feared a worldwide famine. Some people thought the EPA's power should be reduced. Some even suggested all environmental laws should be eliminated. One of the biggest critics, Representative William R. Poage of Texas, fought to weaken the EPA. His office released a statement claiming, "I doubt that very [many] people will give much thought to a clean environment if they are about to starve to death. . . . With the current world population growth rate it is not inconceivable that mass famine will occur in several parts of the world during our generation."[5]

POWER STRUGGLE

The United States was struggling with energy costs as well, especially the cost of the oil and gas used to run cars, heat buildings, and power factories. The Middle Eastern countries and others that produced most of the world's

Gas shortages in the United States in 1973 resulted in long lines to fill up and some gas station closures.

oil demanded higher payments while restricting supply. Gas prices went up. For a short time, gasoline was even rationed in the United States. Alternatives to oil and natural gas such as wind and solar power had not been fully developed, so they were also limited and expensive.

Nuclear power plants were seen as one answer to the energy crisis. They could produce a lot of electric power using uranium rather than burning fossil fuels, making them cheap to operate over the long term. However, they were expensive to build, and the technology came with risks. There was the fear that accidents could result in leaks of dangerous radioactive materials.

In 1979, the Three Mile Island nuclear power plant in Pennsylvania suffered a serious failure. A minor equipment problem set off the chain of events. Because of poorly designed equipment, confusing instruments, and worker errors, the dangerous situation quickly worsened. The accident was largely contained, releasing only a small amount of radiation into the environment. No one was killed or seriously injured, but the accident showed nuclear power was not as safe as assumed. The government made major changes to how it regulated nuclear plants. In 1986, the Chernobyl nuclear power plant in Ukraine had a large accident that caused serious harm to humans and the environment. Despite greater oversight, many people have remained fearful and suspicious of nuclear power. However, in recent years, the fear of climate change from greenhouse gases released by burning fossil fuels has led to new calls for nuclear power.

NUCLEAR DISASTER IN JAPAN

On March 11, 2011, an unprecedented earthquake and tsunami battered Japan at the same time. Most of the reactors at Japan's nuclear power plants shut down safely. However, the tsunami flooded backup generators and other equipment needed to safely shut down three units at the Fukushima Daiichi plant. Radiation leaked into the environment. For several weeks, people struggled to contain the disaster. The destruction from the earthquake and tsunami heightened the challenge.

No deaths have been blamed on the nuclear accident, but thousands of people had to leave their homes in the area around the damaged plant. The disaster once again raised questions about the safety of nuclear power plants.

REACTIONS TO A GROWING POPULATION

A growing population has contributed to the strain on natural resources. Because of medical advancements, more people are being born, and fewer people are dying. The world population grew dramatically in the 1900s. In 1960, the world population was approximately 3 billion. By 1974, a mere 14 years later, an additional billion people had been added.[6] In 2013, world population stood at more than 7 billion.[7]

Two important books addressed the problems of a growing population. *The Population Bomb* by Paul Ehrlich, a biology professor at Stanford University, was published in 1968. It predicted millions of people would starve in the 1970s and 1980s. *The Limits to Growth*, written by a group of researchers from the Massachusetts Institute of Technology,

POPULATION GROWTH

The world population reached 1 billion in 1804. It took 118 years, until 1922, for the population to double to 2 billion. The population grew by another billion in only 37 years. Population growth sped up even more, adding 1 billion people every 12 to 15 years.[8] The population reached 7 billion in 2011.[9]

The world's population is growing by approximately 200,000 people every day.[10] The UN estimates the population will reach approximately 9.3 billion in the year 2050.[11]

claimed many natural resources would run out by the year 2030. Although their worst predictions did not come to pass, these books gave a sense of urgency to the environmental movement.

Other books challenged the idea that bigger and more is always better. *Small Is Beautiful*, written in 1973 by E. F. Schumacher, a British economist, pointed out the dehumanizing effects of big companies. "Any intelligent fool can make things bigger, more complex, and more violent," Schumacher wrote in a companion article. "It takes a touch of genius—and a lot of courage—to move in the opposite direction."[12] Writings such as his caused people to question whether increasing economic growth is always good. Later, the World Commission on Environment and Development released a report introducing the concept of sustainable development. The report suggested poor countries could develop economically while at the same time preserving the environment for future generations.

Another book, *Gaia: A New Look at Life on Earth*, took its name from the Greek goddess of Earth. The book, by British scientist James Lovelock, suggested the planet behaved like a single giant organism. As Lovelock later summarized his theory,

> Just as the shell is part of a snail, so the rocks, the
> air, and the oceans are part of Gaia. Gaia . . . has

Despite earlier predictions, with 7 billion people the Earth has not yet run out of resources.

continuity with the past back to the origins of life, and extends into the future as long as life persists. Gaia, as a total planetary being, has properties that are not necessarily discernible by just knowing individual species or populations of organisms living together.[13]

Many of these texts were looking at environmental problems as global problems that could only be tackled by the coordinated efforts of governments, businesses, and consumers. At the same time, some environmentalists tried to show how the individual could help the environment. People started to learn the individual choices they made, such as where they shopped and what they bought, could make a difference. Over time, more people began to recognize how their everyday actions affected the earth. The notion emerged that people should think globally and act locally. ●

RECYCLING

Recycling is an ancient practice, often used to save money or stretch resources. For example, metal can be melted and reformed into new weapons or tools, a practice thousands of years old. Around 1970, the environmental movement inspired the first curbside recycling in the United States, though the practice was not widespread until the 1990s.

Recycling was one way people began » thinking globally and acting locally.

CHAPTER 5

LOVE CANAL

During the 1970s, people became more aware of how severely humans were polluting the environment. Power stations were releasing sulfur dioxide, which became sulfuric acid in the atmosphere. This acid rain harmed plants and aquatic life. Because it traveled through the air, acid rain could land hundreds of miles away. Acid rain from one country could affect another country, proving once again that pollution had become a global problem. Despite the growing awareness of the dangers of pollution, communities struggled to get officials to

« Hooker Chemical, which was partially responsible for the pollution at Love Canal, was only one of many industries harming the environment at the time.

recognize local problems, let alone fix them. Sometimes people had to work for years to see any change. One battle that brought the dilemma into the public eye was the incident at Love Canal.

A TOWN IN DANGER

Love Canal was a canal begun in 1894 to connect the upper and lower Niagara River near Niagara Falls, New York. The project was never finished, and the partially dug canal became a chemical disposal site from approximately 1920 until 1953. The city of Niagara Falls used the site as a garbage dump. The Hooker Chemical and Plastics Corporation dumped chemical waste, and the US Army dumped chemical warfare material.

In 1953, Hooker Chemical covered the canal and sold the land to the Niagara Falls School Board. Homes were soon built in the area, and an elementary school opened over the old dump. A few years later, the first complaints came in about black sludge, unpleasant smells, and children getting burns from playing in their yards. Despite these warning signs, the government did not investigate until the late 1970s.

The first news reports alerted local residents to the problem in 1978. Articles in the local newspaper listed the chemicals in the canal and possible physical reactions to them, including blood diseases and damage to the central nervous system. No one knew what to do. Lois Gibbs had a son in kindergarten who had developed epilepsy and other health problems. She decided to take a petition around her neighborhood asking for the school built over the canal to be shut down. She was worried people would not listen to her. However, she decided to take action: "What's more important—what people may think or your child's health? Either you're going to do something, or you're going to have to admit you're a coward and not do it."[1]

CUYAHOGA RIVER FIRE

Before the United States had strong environmental protection laws, factories and businesses often dumped their waste into local waters or buried it underground. This could have disastrous results. In June 1969, the Cuyahoga River in Cleveland, Ohio, caught fire. The fire, reported to have reached five stories high at times, lasted approximately 20 minutes before firefighters brought it under control. Investigators determined the fire had been caused by an accumulation of oily waste and debris on the river under two wooden railroad trestles. This fire damaged Cleveland's reputation and brought additional attention to water pollution. The Cuyahoga River was one of the most polluted in the country, contributing to the pollution of Lake Erie. Today, the river is on the rebound. Though the river is still somewhat polluted, government agencies, nonprofit organizations, and volunteers are working to return the Cuyahoga to full health.

Lois Gibbs described her experiences in her 1982 book, *Love Canal: My Story*.

VOICES OF THE MOVEMENT

"As I proceeded down 99th Street, I developed a set speech. I would tell people what I wanted. But the speech wasn't all that necessary. It seemed as though every home on 99th Street had someone with an illness. One family had a young daughter with arthritis. They couldn't understand why she had it at her age. Another daughter had had a miscarriage. The father, still a fairly young man, had had a heart attack. I went to the next house, and there, people would tell me their troubles. People were reaching out; they were telling me their troubles in hopes I would do something. But I didn't know anything to do. I was also confused. I just wanted to stop children from going to that school. Now look at all those other health problems! Maybe they were related to the canal. But even if they were, what could I do?" [2]

Eventually, her neighbors shared their own stories of unexplained illnesses. Many people wanted to move, but they could not sell their homes. Buyers did not want a home near a toxic waste dump.

THE BATTLE CONTINUES

The New York State Health Department held a public meeting to discuss Love Canal, but it provided few answers. Gibbs and her neighbors persisted. They learned everything they could about the situation. They lobbied city and state officials and politicians. They protested at meetings and filed a lawsuit.

The media started paying more attention. The elementary school was closed until the hazards could be removed. The homes closest to the waste dump were evacuated. Some were destroyed without their owners' permission. The New York governor promised to relocate other residents if they could prove their health problems were caused by Love Canal. A map showed a clear relationship between the canal and birth defects, miscarriages, respiratory disorders, and central nervous system problems such as epilepsy. However, no one could definitively prove an individual illness was a result of the substances in the canal.

Gibbs appeared on talk shows and testified before Congress. In the meantime, her two children were

Children protested at a 1978 Love Canal neighborhood meeting.

hospitalized for life-threatening illnesses. Studies showed dangerous toxins in the soil, water, and air around the canal. Love Canal residents continued protesting.

Yet sometimes all the protesters' efforts seemed hopeless. Gibbs reported her feelings after one particularly frustrating experience:

> I said to myself: You can't sit back and shut your mouth, Lois. You aren't the only one they're hurting. They're hurting hundreds of people. You have to get up there and do it, whether you like it or not, whether you have to push yourself or not, whether you stumble or not.[3]

As the protesters grew more desperate, some became violent, stopping cars and setting fire to trees and signs. When EPA officials arrived, the angry crowd took them hostage. Ordinary men and women who had just wanted to raise their families safely had resorted to criminal behavior.

Then, after more than two years of fighting, residents received some good news. They could leave their homes immediately, and the cost would be paid by the federal government. Still, the victory was bittersweet. Some people would never recover from their health problems. They suffered mental and emotional trauma, as well.

HELPING OTHERS

Gibbs moved to Washington, DC, and founded the Citizen's Clearinghouse for Hazardous Wastes. Her goal was to prevent similar problems from happening to other people. The group, later named the Center for Health, Environment and Justice, has assisted more than 8,000 community groups around the country and continues to help communities fight pollution today.[4] Gibbs once said, "Rarely a day goes by that someone hasn't called our office with a terrible, horrible story of tragedy befalling a family member." However, she added, "There are enough wins to balance out the tragedies."[5]

Activist groups now do more than help communities already affected by hazardous waste dumps. They also work to prevent new sites. Thousands of hazardous waste sites existed around the country by the 1970s. Yet no new commercial waste sites have opened

REDUCING CFCS: A SUCCESS STORY

Sometimes small, seemingly innocent objects can cause terrible problems. In 1985, scientists identified a huge hole in the ozone layer. The ozone layer is a region of ozone gas several miles above Earth's surface. This layer protects Earth from the dangerous effects of the sun's ultraviolet rays. Scientists realized it was being depleted by chemicals called chlorofluorocarbons (CFCs) released by people. These chemicals were used as coolants in refrigerators and air conditioning systems and as propellant in spray cans. Governments worldwide agreed to an international treaty to phase out these chemicals in 1987. The ozone layer is now expected to recover. The success of these actions proved that when people worldwide work together quickly, they can solve environmental problems.

since 1982 because they faced too much resistance from the public. Instead, companies have found other ways to deal with the waste, often reusing chemicals or substituting safer ones.

Public health got additional protection in 1980, when Congress passed a new law. The Comprehensive Environmental Response, Compensation, and Liability Act is commonly known as Superfund. This law taxed the chemical and petroleum industries. The tax money went to a trust fund for cleaning up abandoned or uncontrolled hazardous waste sites. It also gave the federal government authority to respond to the release or threatened release of hazardous substances to protect the public.

Love Canal helped bring the environmental movement to the mainstream. It affected everyday people: blue-collar workers and stay-at-home moms who had trusted the government to protect them. People began understanding environmental protection was not only about exotic animals and national parks. Human health and safety were also at stake in local communities. ◉

The events at Love Canal launched Lois Gibbs, *front* »
center, into a career as an environmental activist.

CHAPTER 6

FIGHTING ON MANY FRONTS

A s the world learned about tragedies such as Love Canal, people began understanding how human life is connected to the environment. However, the Green movement still had detractors. Environmental issues often seemed to come down to a battle between activists and businesses. Businesses worried that new regulations would hurt their profitability. In addition, consumers complained when environmental regulation increased the cost of purchasing goods.

When human health was not an issue, the battles to protect nature were often even longer and more difficult. To the animal lover, saving an endangered species may seem a straightforward choice. Yet it can be hard to get everyone to agree. Environmentalists have often come into conflict with people who are worried about jobs or the economy. One of many examples involved the spotted owl.

Spotted owls live in the forests of the Pacific Northwest. The huge trees where they nest are popular with the logging industry. Because of logging, only 10 percent of these old-growth forests remained at the beginning of the 1990s.[1] The number of spotted owls had shrunk as well, due to the loss of their habitat.

In 1986, an environmental group tried to get protection for the spotted owl as an endangered species. After four years of negotiation and legal challenges, the spotted owl was declared threatened under the Endangered Species Act. Biologists estimated approximately 2,000 pairs remained in the early 1990s.[2] The new legal protections did not stop logging, but they placed limits on it. The timber industry asserted the limits would cause people to lose their jobs. It said the mills that

THE NEW ZOO

Many environmentalists fight to protect wild species. As the environmental movement developed, many people wanted to go beyond saving animal lives. How animals were treated—their comfort and happiness—also became important.

The first public zoos opened in the early 1800s, allowing city people to view wild animals from around the world. Early zoos often put animals in small, bare cages. Most zoos simply put animals on display, although a few also did research.

Modern zoos make a serious effort to mimic the animals' natural environments. Zoo workers encourage animals to play, explore, and socialize. Today's zoos study animal health and behavior. They help wildlife conservation efforts and breed rare animals in hopes of keeping the species alive. Some animals are now extinct in the wild and live only in zoos. Zoo animals also help educate the public. By seeing these animals up close, people get more interested in protecting wild species. Zoos can play a big role in protecting wild animals.

processed the trees would close, putting thousands of people out of work.

Environmentalists, on the other hand, argued those jobs would disappear anyway as forests vanished. They asked the timber industry to look for other ways to preserve jobs, such as keeping the processing work in the United States rather than selling raw lumber overseas to be processed there. They said people had a responsibility to protect animal rights, regardless of the cost. Despite legal protection, spotted owls are still considered threatened, and their numbers are slowly declining. The government issued new recovery plans in 2008 and 2011 to reduce habitat loss and protect the owls.

MAKING A POINT

Some environmental groups began taking extreme action to prove their points on various issues. Greenpeace had been founded in 1971 as an antinuclear organization. It soon focused on another goal, ending whaling. Whales had been hunted since the 1800s for their meat, blubber (used to make oil), and baleen, a horny material from the whale's mouth used in fans or corsets. In the mid-1900s, new technology such as faster and bigger boats and explosive harpoons made whalers more successful. Several whale species went into serious decline. For example, it was thought fewer than 5,000 blue whales were left in the world in the 1970s.[3]

Greenpeace members did more than simply sign petitions or lobby the government. Starting in 1973, activists took to the sea and began confronting whaling fleets. They put themselves in between the whalers' harpoons and the whales. These young radicals got the name "eco-warriors."[4]

They caught the media's attention, and soon images of whaling violence hit television. For many people, seeing footage of the slaughter was more powerful than simply hearing numbers. In 1982, the International Whaling

ONGOING THREATS TO WHALES

Whales no longer face extinction from whaling. International treaties to protect whale populations are coordinated by the International Whaling Commission. However, other environmental dangers affect them. As ocean habitat is degraded by pollution in some areas, food supplies drop. Whales can die in collisions with ships. Some scientists believe shipping noise may interfere with whales' ability to navigate. These concerns have not been studied extensively, making it difficult to judge how serious the risks are or how to mitigate them.

Commission agreed to stop commercial whaling, effective in 1986. While some nations still carry out limited whaling for scientific purposes, most whaling stopped. Whale species rebounded, though some, including the blue whale, are still considered to be endangered.

Other organizations also used dramatic actions to attract attention to a cause. People for the Ethical Treatment of Animals (PETA) was founded in 1980 to defend the rights of all animals. PETA challenged people to stop wearing fur, stop eating meat, and stop testing products on animals. Many of their more extreme practices have been controversial. An ad comparing caged animals to Holocaust victims was considered so offensive it was banned by Germany's High Court. Other ads have been called too violent or too sexualized, and some

PETA members staged a protest against automakers using animals in crash tests in 1992.

have been rejected or taken down by television stations, magazines, and billboard companies.

As environmentalists used more aggressive tactics, their opponents fought back, sometimes with violence. Fernando Perreira, a photographer on a Greenpeace ship protesting French nuclear testing in the Pacific Ocean, was killed when French agents blew up the ship in 1985. Chico Mendes, the head of Brazil's National Council of Rubber Tappers, was another victim of violence. Mendes tried to arrange for land in Brazil to be set aside for extractive reserves, meaning the forest would be kept healthy while local people harvested products such as nuts and rubber. In 1988, ranchers who had claimed some of the land shot

Tropical forests include rain forests, with heavy rain year-round; moist forests with heavy seasonal rains; and drier woodlands. All these types of forests are common near the equator, but all are shrinking.

Humans are the major cause of vanishing forests. People clear land to make room for farms and pastures. They cut trees to get wood for construction and fuel. They clear forests to make room for roads and towns. This deforestation can be devastating to other species. Tropical forests cover approximately 7 percent of the earth's dry land, but they may contain half of all species.[7] Deforestation can lead to the extinction of these rare species, some of which may have unknown benefits to humans, such as disease-fighting properties.

Deforestation can also impact the climate. Removing forests affects evaporation and rainfall, which may create a hotter, drier climate. In addition, people often clear forests with fire, releasing carbon stored in the wood. This contributes to greenhouse gases and global warming.

Mendes to death. He was just one of 982 activists killed in land disputes in the Amazon between 1964 and 1988, most by ranchers.[5]

Despite these tragedies, environmentalists prevailed in some cases. By 1998, the Brazilian government had set aside approximately 7.5 million acres (3 million ha) of the Amazon as extractive reserves.[6] The government also cut subsidies it had been providing to help cattle ranchers buy land in the Amazon rain forest. In some regions, deforestation nearly stopped. The battle continues, however. Although Brazil

People have cleared wide swaths of the Amazon rain forest.

dramatically reduced deforestation from 2005 to 2011, 2012 saw the rate of deforestation increase. Changes to Brazilian law and poor law enforcement may be to blame.

Throughout the 1980s, environmental organizations acted to protect nature and conserve resources in a variety of ways. For example, Greenpeace members intervened to stop the dumping of hazardous waste into the sea. Other groups opposed pollution on land and in the air. The green movement was growing, moving into the mainstream of local, national, and global decision making. ●

Greenpeace members dressed as animals »
staged a protest in London, England, over
tropical hardwood forest logging in 2002.

CHAPTER 7

CLIMATE CHANGE TAKES CENTER STAGE

I n the new millennia, one environmental concern has
come to the forefront: climate change. Greenhouse
gases in the atmosphere help keep our planet warm.
They occur naturally from volcanoes, forest fires, and
seepage from cracks in the earth. Without them, the earth
would not be warm enough to support life. However,
increases in the amount of greenhouse gases could cause

the planet to become too warm. Earth's average surface temperature has increased by more than 1.4 degrees Fahrenheit (2.5°C) over the last century. Much of the increase has taken place in the past 35 years.[1]

Greenhouse gases include carbon dioxide, methane, nitrous oxide, and water vapor. These gases become trapped in the atmosphere and prevent heat from escaping into space. These gases stay in the atmosphere anywhere from a few years to hundreds of years. While all of these gases occur naturally, humans have contributed to increasing their atmospheric levels.

In particular, burning fossil fuels has increased the concentration of many greenhouse gases. Fossil fuels include coal, oil, and natural gas, which are used in cars, planes, ships, homes, factories, and electric power plants. The burning of forests also adds carbon dioxide to the atmosphere. Carbon dioxide levels remained steady for approximately 2,000 years before rising during the Industrial Revolution, beginning in the late 1800s. Today atmospheric carbon dioxide concentrations are nearly 40 percent higher than those preindustrial levels.[2] Other greenhouse gases have also increased due to human activity. These activities include methane emissions from raising livestock, using fertilizer, and engaging in industrial processes. Nitrous oxide has increased by

GLOBAL TEMPERATURES

A one or two degree change in temperature might not be noticeable on a daily basis. However, it can make a big difference in global average temperatures. The global average during the last ice age was only nine degrees Fahrenheit (5°C) less than today's average temperature.[4] Yet, at that time much of the world was covered in ice.

The climate is affected by many natural cycles. El Niño and La Niña are periods of natural warming and cooling in the tropical Pacific Ocean. These effects can cause extreme weather, such as flooding and droughts. El Niño is associated with higher temperatures, while La Niña years typically have lower temperatures. However, these small fluctuations are separate from the overall warming trend of the 1900s.

approximately 15 percent since 1750, largely due to fertilizer use.[3]

Scientists measure Earth's temperature on land, in the water, and from satellites. They can tell how warm the climate was in the past for thousands of years by looking at layers of glacial ice drilled out from the Arctic or Antarctica. They also look at other factors to determine how Earth's temperature is changing. For example, glaciers and ice caps are melting around the world. Heat waves have become more frequent, while cold snaps have become shorter and milder on average. Animal and plant species have moved to cooler regions. Many of these things are attributed to global warming.

DANGERS OF A WARMER WORLD

This global warming potentially could have many negative effects. A hotter, drier climate in parts of the world could lead to droughts and an increase in wildfires. Farmers in some areas could have trouble growing food. Many species could go extinct as their habitats change.

While parts of the world become drier, other parts may become wetter. Global warming changes rainfall patterns, causing bigger storms and flooding in some areas. Asia had only 50 floods in the 1950s. In the 1990s, the continent experienced 325 floods.[5] Meanwhile, the Sahara Desert region in Africa is getting as little as half the rainfall the area used to get. In that already dry climate, less rain means fewer crops and more starvation.

GLOBAL WARMING VERSUS CLIMATE CHANGE

Two terms are often used when discussing the changes to the world's climate. Global warming refers to the average temperature increase on Earth's surface caused by greenhouse gases created by people. Climate change is a broader term. It includes global warming and everything else caused by increasing greenhouse gases, such as changes to weather patterns and the rise in sea levels.

The term *global warming* can be confusing to nonscientists, who may assume the phrase means that all temperatures should be warmer year-round. In reality, an increase in the average global temperature can create erratic weather patterns.

With glaciers, ice sheets, and sea ice melting, the sea level is rising. Warmer water also expands, so higher water temperatures lead to even higher sea levels. Since 1870, the average sea level has risen approximately eight inches (20 cm).[6] If this rise continues, as scientists predict, it could cause coastal flooding. That might affect between 5 million and 200 million people worldwide.[7] Most of the world's population lives near coasts, including 50 percent of Americans.[8] US cities including Miami, Florida; New Orleans, Louisiana; and New York City, New York, could be partially underwater. Amsterdam in the Netherlands, Shanghai in China, and the Philippines are also at risk. In the country of Bangladesh and the city of Calcutta, India, 60 million people could lose their homes.[9] Some entire island nations could become unlivable, especially among the Pacific Islands. High-risk islands include the Maldives, Barbados, the Solomon Islands, Papua New Guinea, and Micronesia. Warmer water on the surface of the ocean may also cause larger and more frequent hurricanes. In recent years, the number and severity of hurricanes and typhoons has increased. Hurricanes have also been seen in parts of the world that rarely had them in the past.

« Melting glaciers are one indication of global warming.

BRINGING CLIMATE CHANGE TO THE PUBLIC

Many environmental movements were started when members of the public took an interest in saving an endangered animal or cleaning up a polluted location. In contrast, concerns over climate change began in the scientific community. The first scientific studies on carbon dioxide in the atmosphere were published in the 1950s. In 1988, the Intergovernmental Panel on Climate Change (IPCC) was formed. Its mission is to provide the world's governments with a scientific understanding of climate change and its potential impact. The IPCC has 195 member countries, and it is endorsed by the UN. Thousands of scientists contribute research for review, and each report is compiled by a group of experts.

In 1990, the first IPCC Assessment Report stated that climate change was a topic needing attention. Later reports continued addressing the issue. The IPCC's Climate Change 2007 report brought the world's attention to climate change.

The public started hearing more about climate change. One public voice was Al Gore, who served as US vice president from 1993 to 2001 under President Bill Clinton. Gore had a longtime interest in environmental issues. In an introduction to the 1992 edition of *Silent Spring*, he wrote that Rachel Carson's book was one his family read and discussed around the dinner table:

Rachel Carson was one of the reasons why I became so conscious of the environment and so involved with environmental issues. . . . Her picture hangs on my office wall among those of the political leaders, the presidents and the prime ministers. . . . Carson has had as much or more effect on me than any of them, and perhaps than all of them together.[10]

Gore began giving a slide show about global warming, which became a documentary film in 2006 called *An Inconvenient Truth.*

A SCIENTIST SPEAKS UP

Many scientists are studying climate change. One strong voice is James Hansen, director of the NASA Goddard Institute for Space Studies. He testified before the US Senate in 1988, warning of the dangers if people remained dependent on fossil fuels.

In one study, published in 2012, Hansen and colleagues compared global temperatures of the past 30 years against the prior 30 years. They found far more extreme weather events, such as severe heat waves. Hansen suggested global warming is to blame for some of the extreme weather experienced in recent years.

In a 2012 opinion piece for the *Washington Post*, Hansen wrote, "Extremely hot temperatures covered about 0.1 percent to 0.2 percent of the globe in the base period of our study, from 1951 to 1980. In the last three decades, while the average temperature has slowly risen, the extremes have soared and now cover about 10 percent of the globe."[11] According to Hansen, climate change is not a possible danger of the future. It is already happening.

VOICES OF THE MOVEMENT

Former vice president Al Gore has spread his message about global warming in many formats, including a slide show, a movie, and books for adults and children. As he wrote in 2006 in *An Inconvenient Truth: The Planetary Emergency of Global Warming and What We Can Do About It*:

"Yes, the science is ongoing and always evolving, but there's already enough data, enough damage, to know without question that we're in trouble. This isn't an ideological debate with two sides, pro and con. There is only one Earth, and all of us who live on it share a common future. Right now we are facing a planetary emergency, and it is time for action."[12]

Al Gore's presentations raised public awareness about global warming and climate change.

Although some data in his slide show and later books has been challenged, most is accepted by scientists, and Gore is credited with raising public awareness of climate change. The IPCC and Al Gore won the 2007 Nobel Peace Prize on December 10 for their work.

Reacting to issues including climate change, the environmental movement began to focus on science and research. The spiritual metaphors of Muir and Thoreau, while still inspiring to some environmentalists, were not enough to convince the public or government to change policies. Around the world, scientists have come to agree climate change is a problem and it is caused by human activities. Arguments continue about how best to address the issue, but many governments, businesses, and individuals have come to agree major changes are needed. Other scientists are looking into ways to adapt to the climate changes that have already begun occurring.

Researchers study changes in Antarctica to try » to understand the effects of global warming.

CHAPTER 8

MANY GROUPS, MANY GOALS

Some social change movements have a single primary goal. For example, the suffragists wanted the vote for women. The Green movement, on the other hand, is far from a single movement with a single path. Instead, it is made up of thousands of groups working toward thousands of individual goals. By one estimate, approximately 30,000 environmental organizations are active around the world today.[1]

Some groups have been around for more than a century. Others spring up when needed and disappear after completing a specific task, such as preventing a toxic waste dump.

The Green movement is also closely tied with other social change movements. When a company dumps toxic waste in a river, it is a health issue. When a government allows mining on land belonging to native groups, human rights issues are at stake. When electric companies charge more for solar and wind power, it is a consumer issue as well as an energy issue. When the population grows so large there is not enough food for everyone, poverty and environmental issues meet.

This makes the environmental

CREATIVE BATTLES

Many environmental groups spring up when someone sees a problem and wants to solve it. Around the world, small groups fight for change in creative ways. In Brazil, a group led by Rodrigo Baggio takes discarded computers from other countries. The organization uses them to teach computer skills to poor children, combining recycling and education. In India, Sumita Dasgupta leads a group on trips to study ancient systems for catching rainwater. Dasgupta's group hopes to use these systems to counter drought. Many successful groups focus on small, immediate actions that have clear results.

movement large, long lasting, and complex. An animal rights group may want to stop hunting. A sportsman's group may want to ensure there is enough wildlife for hunting. Both groups could broadly be considered part of the environmental movement.

Different groups may also band together to fight for the same cause. One group may want to stop a proposed mining operation because of the ugly scars it will leave on the land. Another group may be concerned about the mining pollution affecting human health. A third group may want to protect their sacred religious spots. With so many different priorities, groups will sometimes disagree.

THINK GLOBALLY, ACT LOCALLY

The Green movement reaches from the international to the local level. Participants may do work at many levels, from recycling or composting their

DEFINING GOALS

Environmental groups can be broken into categories. Watch organizations work as monitors, inspecting a specific place, corporation, or project. Friends organizations are more hands-on; they may help clean up and improve natural places. Other groups may be called defenders, coalitions, or alliances and advocate positions before regulators, courts, and legislators. These terms help identify the goals of various groups.

household trash to donating to charities protecting wildlife in Africa. One often heard mantra is "Think Globally, Act Locally." This promotes the idea that in order to solve global environmental problems, individuals should focus on what they can do at home and in their own communities.

A person does not have to belong to a formal group to be part of the Green movement. Individuals and families can take action on their own. People can use more energy-efficient lightbulbs and turn off lights when they are not in use. They can turn off or unplug electronic devices to reduce power use. They can choose to drive fuel-efficient cars or even cars that do not depend on gasoline.

NO IMPACT MAN

Colin Beavan's family attempted to spend a year living in New York City while causing no net environmental impact. Over the course of the year, Colin and his wife researched their options and tried to reduce damage in one area at a time. To reduce their power consumption, they did not use vehicles, elevators, air conditioning, the dishwasher, or television. They bought milk in reusable glass bottles and avoided other products in disposable packaging. Even with these changes, they recognized that it was impossible to do absolutely no environmental harm. To balance out their impact, they included positive actions, such as volunteering with the Nature Conservancy. The experiment became a book and a documentary movie, both called *No Impact Man*.

Taking public transportation, riding bikes, or walking whenever possible are even better for the environment.

To reduce waste, people can use refillable water bottles instead of buying new bottles for every drink. They can avoid buying foods that have a lot of packaging and even grow some of their own food. They can recycle wherever recycling is available. Buying organic foods grown without pesticides is another shopping choice that may benefit the environment. So is buying local produce in season, rather than produce shipped from around the world, which requires more energy for transportation.

People can make a greater impact when they work together. Community groups can start community gardens or build green roofs on public buildings. A green roof is designed to grow plants on top of a building. This helps insulate the building and filter pollutants from the air, and it can even provide food. Communities can protect wild spaces or build parks. A tree will absorb 1 short ton (0.9 metric tons) of carbon dioxide over its lifetime, so maintaining green spaces helps the planet.[2] People can also work together to clean up the land and water in their area.

Local and federal governments can take on larger projects. They can support alternate forms of power, such as wind, solar, or geothermal. They can build public transportation systems that reduce the number of cars

Green roofs beautify buildings while providing insulation and decreasing storm water runoff.

on the road. A bus system could use hydrogen fuel cell buses, which emit exhaust that is water vapor instead of carbon dioxide. The government can undertake research and development that people or nongovernmental organizations cannot. Governments have to balance many concerns, including the economy and a broader energy strategy; the environment is now typically one element that is considered. The cost of a new technology such

Communities must decide if the benefits of energy-saving technology such as hydrogen fuel cell buses are worth the expense.

as a hydrogen fuel cell bus must be weighed against its potential benefits, as well as considered in relation to the government's overall expenses and needs. Individuals and groups can petition the government to include the environment in governmental decisions, regulations, and budgets.

The many environmental groups worldwide allow people to dedicate additional time and money to their special environmental concerns. For example, River Network helps people organize to protect and restore rivers and watersheds. ReefGuardian International attempts to protect coral reefs worldwide. The African

Wildlife Foundation works to protect land and wildlife while empowering local people. Other organizations focus on specific species, such as whales or gorillas. An environmental group exists for just about every interest or cause. Most people are now aware of simple ways to help the environment. This shows how far the environmental movement has reached.

THE BRIDGE TRAGEDY • MURDOCH'S WAR PLAN

Newsweek

Global
Warming Is
A Hoax.*

* Or so claim well-funded
naysayers who still reject the
overwhelming evidence of
climate change. Inside the denial
machine. By Sharon Begley

CHAPTER 9

THE BATTLES
CONTINUE

T
he Green movement faces continuing challenges
to address climate change, pollution, species
loss, and many other environmental concerns.
One challenge for the Green movement is educating
individuals about the science behind climate change and
other environmental problems. Another challenge is how
the issue is portrayed in the press. For example, at least
97 percent of climate scientists agree global warming is

caused by humans.[1] The University of California reviewed ten years' worth of scientific studies on global warming, including more than 900 articles. None of them doubted humans were responsible for global warming. However, in more than 600 articles in the popular press about global warming, more than half expressed doubt as to the causes of global warming.[2]

Some people and companies also worry about the cost of taking care of the environment. People tend to worry more about economic problems that affect them now, rather than climate change that may affect them in the future. According to a 2012 report from the Grantham Research Institute on Climate Change and the Environment at the London School of Economics, "The overall pace of change is recklessly slow. We are acting as if change is too difficult and costly and delay is not a problem."[3]

Reducing human impact on the environment can be more costly in the short term. However, investments in greener sources of power and fuel would likely be cheaper in the long run. Green practices can also have benefits that are not immediately obvious. One study looked at the Canadian province of Nova Scotia, which was recycling 50 percent of its trash. The cost of recycling was

GLOBAL RECYCLING

Worldwide, the recycling industry processes more than 500 million short tons (450 million metric tons) of materials each year. Recycling can dramatically reduce the energy needed to produce a product. For example, aluminum soda cans require approximately one-fifth as much energy when they are recycled as when they are made from scratch. However, some materials are more difficult and more expensive to recycle than others. Recycling also reduces the garbage in landfills, where trash produces greenhouse gases as it decays.[5] One in-depth European study showed in 83 percent of scenarios recycling is better for the environment than burying or burning waste.[6]

People in slums around the world from Brazil to India have improved their standard of living by scavenging recyclables. However, the industry remains a blessing and a curse. People in developing countries such as China who process recyclables, especially electronic waste, are exposed to dangerous chemicals that are likely increasing their risk of cancer.

$18 million more than throwing away the trash. Yet benefits included saving energy by using recycled materials in new products; more jobs in the recycling industry; and benefits to tourism and the property market. In fact, Nova Scotia was saving up to $125 million due to its recycling program.[4] Savings like this allow communities to spend more money on roads, schools, and other needs.

SUPPORTING GREEN

Because of the cost and complexity of many green issues, governments are better positioned to be effective at

Government incentives can encourage people to install solar panels or adopt other energy-saving solutions.

protecting the environment than organizations or individuals. Governmental bodies can pass laws and adopt regulations to reduce pollution, to protect wildlife, and to ensure safe and healthy business practices. The government is necessary to enforce laws to ensure companies do not ignore regulations in favor of cheaper or easier practices. The US government also provides financial help to businesses that develop cleaner energy or

GREENWASHING

Many companies embrace environmentally friendly actions, such as reducing plastic packaging, using solar energy, or donating money to environmental charities. Part of this stems from a sincere desire to do good. But many companies also hope to increase their sales by advertising these products or behaviors. Many consumers will preferentially buy from environmentally conscious companies or even pay more for products claiming to be green.

Unfortunately, some companies claim to be doing more good than they actually are, a practice known as greenwashing. This can cause a consumer backlash if the truth gets out. The US Federal Trade Commission (FTC) investigates some green claims, and in 1992 issued "Guides for the Use of Environmental Marketing Claims." The guidelines defined terms such as *biodegradable* and *recyclable* and laid down principles for advertising. The FTC periodically updates these guides to ensure businesses understand the rules and consumers can trust marketing claims.

manufacturing processes. The government even offers tax savings for individuals who purchase green vehicles or appliances. Sometimes government action originates with elected officials or government employees who believe in environmental causes, while at other times outside environmental organizations pressure the government to act.

Many companies are willingly joining the Green movement because they see these actions as good business. They may be motivated partly by helping the environment and partly by catering to consumer desires for "green" products. Known as the sustainable business movement, the goal is to have a successful business without hurting the environment. Practitioners face many challenges. Even businesses that make green improvements may also increase their environmental damage as they grow to meet new consumer demands.

On an individual level, people often find it difficult to decide what is best for the environment. Is it better to use disposable diapers, which fill up landfills, or cloth diapers, which require water for washing? Paper bags made from trees, plastic bags that may become litter, or biodegradable plastic bags that release greenhouse gases as they decay? Can the adoption of electric cars end air pollution? Electric cars may use less fossil fuel directly, but if they are

ECO-FRIENDLY SHOPPING

According to a 2006 report by a consumer research firm, approximately 35 million Americans regularly buy products that claim to be environmentally friendly.[7] These items may range from organic cotton clothing to hybrid cars. However, some environmentalists warn making better shopping decisions will not have a huge impact on the greater problem. "Buying green" could fool people into thinking they are helping the environment more than they are. Critics of eco-friendly shopping say people should reduce their consumption overall. Still, eco-friendly shopping can be a starting point to get people thinking about the environment.

charged using electricity from coal power plants they may be just shifting the problem. An Internet search on "what's really better for the environment?" will turn up many debates. Uncovering the truth can take time and effort.

Even among environmentalists, opinions differ. There is no one clear, simple path that will allow us to protect the environment while feeding billions of new people. World leaders are discussing the potential of sustainable development. This term typically means development that meets the needs of people now without damaging the ability of future generations to meet their own needs. As a specific example, this involves feeding people without destroying forests for farmland or overfishing the oceans. Sustainable development helps us make choices and form solutions based on competing considerations.

Despite the challenges facing the Green movement, environmentalists can look back on enormous progress. Fifty years ago, few people knew or cared about the problems facing the environment. The term *global warming* was not used until 1975, while climate change became a topic of discussion in 1979. Neither concept was widely understood by the public until decades later. Now there is much greater awareness of the dangers of pollution, deforestation, and climate change. Environmentalists are working with other groups to find solutions that can benefit both people and nature.

Green movement activists continue
pushing for change worldwide.

The struggle to protect the environment is far from over,
but the Green movement has become an important part of
the modern world.

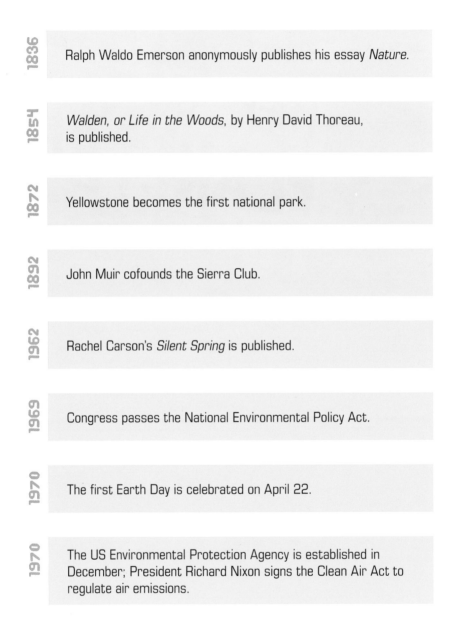

1836 Ralph Waldo Emerson anonymously publishes his essay *Nature*.

1854 *Walden, or Life in the Woods*, by Henry David Thoreau, is published.

1872 Yellowstone becomes the first national park.

1892 John Muir cofounds the Sierra Club.

1962 Rachel Carson's *Silent Spring* is published.

1969 Congress passes the National Environmental Policy Act.

1970 The first Earth Day is celebrated on April 22.

1970 The US Environmental Protection Agency is established in December; President Richard Nixon signs the Clean Air Act to regulate air emissions.

1972 The United States begins banning some pesticides on December 31; the Clean Water Act, governing water pollution, passes.

1973 The Endangered Species Act is signed on December 28.

1978 In June, the first news reports alert people to the dangers of Love Canal.

1988 The Earth Island Institute sets off a nationwide tuna boycott to protest dolphin killings.

1988 The Intergovernmental Panel on Climate Change (IPCC) is established.

2006 Al Gore's documentary, *An Inconvenient Truth*, is released.

2007 The IPCC's Climate Change 2007 report brings the world's attention to climate change.

2011 The world population reaches 7 billion.

GLOBAL WARMING OPINION: 2008–2012

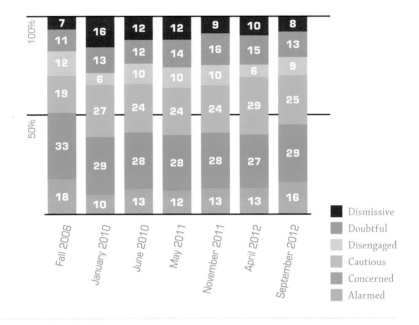

DATE OF THE MOVEMENT'S BEGINNING

1962, with the release of Rachel Carson's *Silent Spring*

LOCATIONS

Love Canal; Three Mile Island; Yosemite National Park

KEY PLAYERS

John Muir cofounded the Sierra Club and lobbied for the national park system.

Biologist **Rachel Carson** wrote *Silent Spring* about the dangers of pesticides.

US RECYCLING RATES: 1960–2010

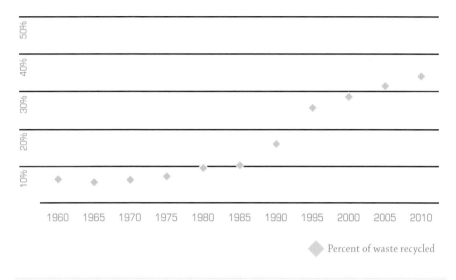

Percent of waste recycled

Senator **Gaylord Nelson** of Wisconsin proposed the first Earth Day, which was held on April 22, 1970.

Al Gore, US vice president from 1993 to 2001, is credited with raising public awareness of climate change through his documentary, *An Inconvenient Truth*.

GOALS AND OUTCOMES

Since the 1800s, environmentalists have worked to preserve wild lands and species and reduce pollution. Especially since the 1960s and the publication of *Silent Spring*, the public has become more aware about environmental damage and what individuals can do to help. The movement continues fighting to slow global warming and climate change.

GLOSSARY

acid rain
Precipitation that contains an unusually high concentration of acid-forming chemicals, such as sulfur, from pollutants released into the air and combined with water vapor.

advocacy
The act of supporting a cause.

conservation
Protecting the environment for the future while allowing human use.

deforestation
The action of clearing an area of forests.

eradicate
Wipe out or do away with.

erratic
Inconsistent or having no fixed pattern.

extolling
Giving high praise.

geothermal
Relating to the heat inside the earth.

industrialization
Developing industry on a large scale.

lobby
To attempt to change a politician's position on an issue.

organic
Relating to living plants and animals; grown without chemical fertilizers or pesticides.

pesticide

A chemical compound for destroying plant, animal, or fungal pests.

preservation

Protecting the environment by preventing human use.

rationing

Restricting the amount of something someone is allowed to have.

sustainability

The capacity of something to be used while also being protected for use in the future.

utilitarian

Designed for function and use.

ADDITIONAL RESOURCES

SELECTED BIBLIOGRAPHY

Carson, Rachel. *Silent Spring*. New York: Houghton, 1962. Print.

Hawken, Paul. *Blessed Unrest*. New York: Viking, 2007. Print.

Kinkela, David. *DDT & the American Century*. Chapel Hill, NC: U of North Carolina P, 2011. Print.

FURTHER READINGS

Miller, Debra A., ed. *The Green Movement*. Detroit, MI: Greenhaven, 2010. Print.

Gillam, Scott. *Rachel Carson: Pioneer of Environmentalism*. Edina, MN: ABDO, 2011. Print.

Wheeler, Benjamin, Gilda Wheeler, and Wendy Church. *It's All Connected: A Comprehensive Guide to Global Issues and Sustainable Solutions*. Seattle, WA: Facing the Future, 2005. Print.

WEB SITES

To learn more about the Green movement, visit ABDO Publishing Company online at **www.abdopublishing.com**. Web sites about the Green movement are featured on our Book Links page. These links are routinely monitored and updated to provide the most current information available.

PLACES TO VISIT

Brooklyn Children's Museum

145 Brooklyn Avenue
Brooklyn, NY 11213
718-735-4400
http://www.brooklynkids.org
The Brooklyn Children's Museum has exhibits on nature.
As part of the Green Threads program, the museum also
provides a map of green locations people can visit throughout
New York City.

John G. Shedd Aquarium

1200 S. Lake Shore Drive
Chicago, IL 60605
312-939-2438
http://www.sheddaquarium.org
Zoos and aquariums allow visitors to view and learn about
animals and their habitats. Chicago's Shedd Aquarium has
exhibits on the Amazon and Caribbean reefs.

Yosemite National Park

Public Information Office
P.O. Box 577
Yosemite, CA 95389
http://www.nps.gov/yose/index.htm
Yosemite National Park in California was one of the first
natural places protected by the US government.

SOURCE NOTES

CHAPTER 1. TAKING ACTION, ONE STEP AT A TIME

1. "Frequently Asked Questions about Mead/Bateson." *Institute for Intercultural Studies*. Institute for Intercultural Studies, n.d. Web. 13 Apr. 2013.

2. "The Tuna-Dolphin Issue." *Southwest Fisheries Science Center*. NOAA Fisheries Service, 6 Nov. 2008. Web. 4 Apr. 2013.

3. "Making Waves." *Los Angeles Times*. Los Angeles Times, 19 Oct. 1989. Web. 4 Apr. 2013.

4. "The Current Mass Extinction." *Evolution*. PBS, 2001. Web. 4 Apr. 2013.

5. "The Extinction Crisis." *Center for Biological Diversity*. Center for Biological Diversity, n.d. Web. 4 Apr. 2013.

6. "Decline and Loss of Species." *United Nations Environmental Programme*. United Nations, 2002. Web. 4 Apr. 2013.

7. Rebecca Lindsey. "Tropical Deforestation." *NASA Earth Observatory*. NASA, 30 Mar. 2007. Web. 4 Apr. 2013.

8. "Samuel LaBudde." *The Goldman Environmental Prize*. Goldman Prize, n.d. Web. 4 Apr. 2013.

9. "Our Story." *Earth Island Institute*. Earth Island Institute, 2008. Web. 4 Apr. 2013.

CHAPTER 2. FROM TAMING THE WILDERNESS TO PROTECTING IT

1. J. David Archibald. "Dinosaur Extinction: Changing Views." *Dinosaurs: The Science Behind the Stories*. PDF. 99–100. Web. 14 Dec 2012.

2. Ralph Waldo Emerson. "Nature." *The Prose Works of Ralph Waldo Emerson*. Boston, 1870. 8. *Google Book Search*. Web. 4 Apr. 2013.

3. Henry David Thoreau. *Walden*. New York: Crowell, 1910. 170. *Google Book Search*. Web. 4 Apr. 2013.

4. Paul Hawken. *Blessed Unrest*. New York: Viking, 2007. Print. 40.

5. "About the National Parks." *National Parks Conservation Association*. National Parks Conservation Association, n.d. Web. 4 Apr. 2013.

6. "About the Sierra Club." *Sierra Club*. Sierra Club, n.d. Web. 4 Apr. 2013.

7. Ibid.

8. John Muir. "The American Forests." *Atlantic*. Atlantic, 1 Aug. 1897. Web. 4 Apr. 2013.

9. "Theodore Roosevelt." *The National Parks*. PBS, 2009. Web. 4 Apr. 2013.

CHAPTER 3. THE MODERN ENVIRONMENTAL MOVEMENT

1. David Kinkela. *DDT and the American Century*. Chapel Hill: U of North Carolina P, 2011. Print. 92.

2. Ibid. 94.

3. Ibid. 182.

4. "Rachel Carson: The Green Revolutionary." *The Independent.* The Independent, 11 June 2012. Web. 4 Apr. 2013.

5. Dorothy McLaughlin. "Fooling with Nature: Silent Spring Revisited." *Frontline*. PBS, 2 June 1998. Web. 4 Apr. 2013.

6. Al Gore. Introduction. *Silent Spring*. By Rachel Carson. New York: Houghton, 1994. Print. xvii.

7. Rachel Carson. *Silent Spring*. New York: Houghton, 1994. Print. 2.

8. David Kinkela. *DDT and the American Century*. Chapel Hill: U of North Carolina P, 2011. Print. 172

9. "The Guardian: Origins of the EPA." *EPA Historical Publication*. EPA, 1992. Web. 4 Apr. 2013.

10. "About the Peregrine Fund." *Peregrine Fund.* Peregrine Fund, n.d. Web. 4 Apr. 2013.

11. "Earth Day: The History of the Movement." *Earth Day Network*. Earth Day Network, n.d. Web. 4 Apr. 2013.

12. Ibid.

13. Bill Christofferson. *The Man from Clear Lake: Earth Day Founder Senator Gaylord Nelson*. Madison: U of Wisconsin P, 2010. 533. *Google Book Search*. Web. 4 Apr. 2013.

14. Jack Lewis. "The Birth of EPA." *EPA Journal*. EPA, Nov. 1985. Web. 4 Apr. 2013.

CHAPTER 4. GREEN GOES GLOBAL

1. "Basic Sources: Declaration of the United Nations Conference on the Human Environment." *EISIL*. Electronic Information System for International Law, n.d. Web. 4 Apr. 2013.

2. "Declaration of the United Nations Conference on the Human Environment." *United Nations Environment Programme*. UN, 16 June 1972. Web. 4 Apr. 2013.

3. David Kinkela. *DDT and the American Century*. Chapel Hill: U of North Carolina P, 2011. Print. 167.

4. Ibid. 173.

5. Ibid. 170.

6. "Global Population Profile: 2002." *US Census Bureau*. US Census Bureau, 2002. 11. PDF. 4 Apr. 2013.

7. "US and World Population Clocks." *US Census Bureau*. US Census Bureau, 2013. Web. 4 Apr. 2013.

8. "Global Population Profile: 2002." *US Census Bureau*. US Census Bureau, 2002. 11. PDF. 4 Apr. 2013.

9. "Human Population Reaches 7 Billion." *Scientific American*. Scientific American, 27 Oct. 2011. Web. 4 Apr. 2013.

10. "Population Growth Rate." *DEPWeb*. World Bank, 2001. Web. 4 Apr. 2013.

11. Michael McCarthy. "The Green Movement at 50." *The Independent*. The Independent, 15 June 2012. Web. 4 Apr. 2013.

12. E. F. Schumacher. "Small Is Beautiful." *Radical Humanist* 37 (1973): 22. *Google Book Search*. Web. 5 Apr. 2013.

13. James Lovelock. *The Ages of Gaia*. Reissued. New York: Oxford UP, 2000. *Google Book Search*. Web. 5 Apr. 2013.

CHAPTER 5. LOVE CANAL

1. Aubrey Wallace. *Eco-Heroes*. San Francisco, CA: Mercury, 1993. Print. 171.

2. Lois Marie Gibbs. *Love Canal: My Story*. Albany: State U of New York P, 1982. 15. *Google Book Search*. Web. 4 Apr. 2013.

3. Aubrey Wallace. *Eco-Heroes*. San Francisco, CA: Mercury, 1993. Print. 178.

4. "Lois Gibbs." *The Goldman Environmental Prize*. Goldman Prize, n.d. Web. 4 Apr. 2013.

5. *The Goldman Environmental Prize*. Goldman Prize, n.d. Web. 4 Apr. 2013. 168.

CHAPTER 6. FIGHTING ON MANY FRONTS

1. Claire Andre and Manuel Velasquez. "Ethics and the Spotted Owl Controversy." *Markkula Center for Applied Ethics*. Santa Clara University, 1991. Web. 4 Apr. 2013.

2. Ibid.

3. Michael McCarthy. "A Badge of Honour: The Fight to Save the Whale." *The Independent*. The Independent, 13 June 2012. Web. 4 Apr. 2013.

4. Ibid.

5. "Chico Mendes's Legacy." *New York Times*. New York Times, 26 Dec. 1998. Web. 4 Apr. 2013.

6. Ibid.

7. Rebecca Lindsey. "Tropical Deforestation." *NASA Earth Observatory*. NASA, 30 Mar. 2007. Web. 4 Apr. 2013.

CHAPTER 7. CLIMATE CHANGE TAKES CENTER STAGE

1. "Climate Change: Evidence, Impacts, and Choices." *National Research Council*. National Academy of Science, 2012. 3. PDF. 4 Apr. 2013.

2. Ibid.

3. Ibid.

4. Ibid.

5. Al Gore. *An Inconvenient Truth: The Planetary Emergency of Global Warming and What We Can Do About It*. Emmaus, PA: Rodale, 2006. Print. 106.

6. "Climate Change: Evidence, Impacts, and Choices." *National Research Council*. National Academy of Science, 2012. 15. PDF. 4 Apr. 2013.

7. Ibid.

8. "Rising Seas." *A Student's Guide to Global Climate Change*. EPA, 30 Oct. 2012. Web. 4 Apr. 2013.

9. Al Gore. *An Inconvenient Truth: The Planetary Emergency of Global Warming and What We Can Do About It*. Emmaus, PA: Rodale, 2006. Print. 206.

10. Al Gore. Introduction. *Silent Spring*. By Rachel Carson. New York: Houghton, 1994. Print. xviii.

11. James E. Hansen. "Climate Change Is Here." *Washington Post*. Washington Post, 3 Aug. 2012. Web. 4 Apr. 2013.

12. Al Gore. *An Inconvenient Truth: The Planetary Emergency of Global Warming and What We Can Do About It*. Emmaus, PA: Rodale, 2006. Print. 287.

CHAPTER 8. MANY GROUPS, MANY GOALS

1. Paul Hawken. *Blessed Unrest*. New York: Viking, 2007. Print. 2.

2. "Take Action Now." *An Inconvenient Truth*. Take Part, n.d. Web. 4 Apr. 2013.

CHAPTER 9. THE BATTLES CONTINUE

1. "Surveyed Scientists Agree Global Warming Is Real." *CNN*. CNN, 20 Jan. 2009. Web. 4 Apr. 2013.

2. Al Gore. *An Inconvenient Truth: The Planetary Emergency of Global Warming and What We Can Do About It*. Emmaus, PA: Rodale, 2006. Print. 163.

3. "'Recklessly Slow' Climate Talks as Greenhouse Gases Hit New High." *The Independent*. The Independent, 3 Dec. 2012. Web. 4 Apr. 2013.

4. "All About: Recycling." *CNN*. CNN, 4 Feb. 2008. Web. 4 Apr. 2013.

5. Ibid.

6. "The Truth about Recycling." *Economist*. Economist, 7 June 2007. Web. 4 Apr. 2013.

7. "Green Living." *Mintel*. Mintel, Sep. 2006. Web. 4 Apr. 2013.

INDEX

ABOUT THE AUTHOR

Chris Eboch writes about science, history, and culture for all ages. Her novels for young people include historical fiction, ghost stories, and action-packed adventures. Learn more at www.chriseboch.com.

ABOUT THE CONSULTANT

James E. Hickey Jr. is professor of law at Maurice A. Deane School of Law at Hofstra University where he teaches energy, natural resources, and international law courses. He has practiced energy and international law with two Washington, DC, law firms. He is past chair of the ABA Special Committee on Electric Industry Restructuring. He sits on the Book Publications Board of the ABA Section of Environment, Energy and Resources and is a fellow of the American Bar Foundation. He has more than 60 publications, including the books *Energy Law and Policy for the 21st Century* (2000) and *The Environment: Global Problems, Local Solutions* (1994). He has visited and taught at numerous universities around the world.